YUMMY HEALTHY DINNERS

The easy, guilt-free solution to look good, feel great, and
always know what to have for dinner.

By Jason Rosell

Look good, feel great and enjoy healthy, delicious, and simple dinner recipes!

After a long, stressful day, it is frustrating not knowing what to eat for dinner. Many of us mess up the "diet" by overeating or making unhealthy food choices. These recipes are designed for the super busy person who wants to lose weight and get in shape but doesn't have a lot of time to prepare yummy, healthy dinners.

After many years of being overweight, these are the dinners that helped me reach and maintain my own health and fitness goals. I've used my personal experience and meal plans to help thousands of clients attain and keep a healthy lifestyle all while enjoying themselves each time they have a flavorful dinner.

In this book, you'll find my favorite two weeks' worth of quick and easy recipes (including a weekly cheat day) for a variety of delicious dishes. After two weeks, simply repeat the dinner menus and you will have healthy meals for an entire month! I take away the guesswork involved in healthy, tasty meal planning, and save you money by preventing you from eating out. More importantly, you will have fun preparing and eating delicious dinners that can be completed in minutes!

My Yummy Healthy Dinners plan can be customized to your specific goals by increasing or reducing the amount of protein specified in the recipes. Additionally, if there are any ingredients that you allergic to or simply don't enjoy, just eliminate or replace them to suit your individual needs and medical conditions. Most of the recipe portions listed within the book are for 1 person so feel free to double or increase the portions according to your particular family meal needs. I want you to get creative, have fun and enjoy Yummy Healthy Dinners to the max!

Are you ready to get started?!

With love,

Jason

TABLE OF CONTENTS

CHICKEN CAULIFLOWER FAJITAS

Serves 1

INGREDIENTS

olive oil cooking spray

1/4 sliced red pepper (raw)

1/4 sliced yellow pepper (raw)

3-4 ounces of chicken breast

2 cauliflower tortilla wraps (I recommend Caulipower brand)

Seasoning: Feel free to use any sodium free seasonings to enhance taste. My personal favorite is the brand "Mrs. Dash."

DIRECTIONS

1. Slice peppers and chicken into small strips.

2. In a frying pan, spray olive oil cooking spray until pan is completely covered.

3. Place peppers into pan and cook on medium-high for 5-6 minutes while stirring until tender.

4. After the peppers are cooked, place the chicken strips into frying pan and cook together with the peppers for another 5-6 minutes depending on how you like your chicken cooked.

5. Place cooked peppers and chicken into the cauliflower wrap. Serve and enjoy!

CALIENTE TIP:
Add some jalapenos and 1 teaspoon of salsa on top for even more flavor!

APPROXIMATE MACROS

Calories....................260
Proteins.................27.5g
Fats.........................4g
Carbs.....................24g

STEAK CAULIFLOWER FAJITAS

Serves 1

INGREDIENTS

olive oil cooking spray

3-4 ounces lean flank steak

1/4 sliced red pepper (raw)

1/4 sliced yellow pepper (raw)

1/4 sliced onion (raw)

2 cauliflower tortilla wraps (I recommend Caulipower brand)

Seasoning: Feel free to use any sodium free seasonings to enhance taste. My personal favorite is the brand "Mrs. Dash."

DIRECTIONS

1. Slice peppers and steak into small strips.

2. In a frying pan, spray olive oil cooking spray until pan is completely covered.

3. Place peppers into pan and cook on medium-high for 5-6 minutes while stirring until tender.

4. After the peppers are cooked, place the steak strips into frying pan and cook together with the peppers for another 5-6 minutes depending on how you like your steak cooked.

5. Place cooked peppers and steak into the cauliflower wrap. Serve and enjoy!

CALIENTE TIP:

Add some jalapenos and 1 teaspoon of salsa on top for even more flavor.
Use 1 teaspoon of steak sauce for even more of a kick!

APPROXIMATE MACROS

Calories......................305
Proteins..................26g
Fats........................8g
Carbs....................24g

VEGGIE CAULIFLOWER PIZZA

Serves 1

INGREDIENTS

1 "Caulipower" brand veggie pizza
(my personal favorite style)

DIRECTIONS

1. Keep your CAULIPOWER pizza frozen
as you preheat the oven to 425° F. Bake
for 13-15 minutes or until crust is crispy
and cheese is golden-brown.

2. Cut in half.

3. Serve and enjoy half of pizza with a lot
less calories!

APPROXIMATE MACROS

Calories......................310
Proteins..................10g
Fats.........................14g
Carbs......................37g

CALIENTE TIP:
Add sliced olives and jalapenos along
with hot sauce for an extra kick!

SHRIMP LINGUINI ZUCCHINI

Serves 1

INGREDIENTS

2 cups of spiralized zucchini (find it already pre made at local super market)

1 teaspoon of minced garlic

olive oil cooking spray

12 medium shrimp – fresh or unfrozen (Only 7 calories per shrimp!)

1 lemon

DIRECTIONS

1. In a frying pan, spray olive oil cooking spray until pan is completely covered.

2. Place the zucchini and minced garlic into pan on medium-high for 5 minutes while stirring.

3. Place shrimp into pan and cook on medium-high while stirring for another 5 minutes.

4. Once done cooking, put on plate, and add desired lemon juice on top.
Serve and enjoy!

APPROXIMATE MACROS

Calories......................188
Proteins..................27g
Fats.........................0.7g
Carbs......................18g

CALIENTE TIP:
Sprinkle some parmesan cheese on top for flavor!

APPROXIMATE MACROS

Calories......................235
Proteins...................31.5g
Fats..........................5.5g
Carbs.......................37g

PROTEIN STUFFED PEPPERS

Serves 3

INGREDIENTS

3 large full peppers (red, orange and yellow)

¼ red chopped pepper

1 lb. 96% lean ground beef

1 cup cilantro

¼ onion chopped

½ can no salt tomato sauce

olive oil cooking spray

low sodium salt

DIRECTIONS

1. Cut off the tops of all peppers; discard seeds and membranes.

2. In a deep skillet, spray olive cooking spray until pan is completely covered.

3. In the skillet, cook the onion, cilantro and chopped pepper on medium-high for 5 minutes.

4. Now add tomato sauce and ground beef to the same skillet with the cooked veggies. Cook for another 10 minutes while stirring until it is all evenly cooked.

5. Add desirable seasonings and 1 teaspoon of low sodium salt. Stir all ingredients well.

6. Bake in a 350-degree oven for 30 minutes. Serve and enjoy!

CALIENTE TIP:
You can replace ground beef with ground turkey, chicken or veal.

BURGER LETTUCE WRAP

Serves 1

INGREDIENTS

1 96% lean beef hamburger or 1 lean turkey burger

1 large lettuce leaf. Use romaine lettuce or butter lettuce

2 tablespoons of no salt ketchup

1 teaspoon of low sodium salt

pinch of black pepper

olive oil cooking spray

Seasoning: Feel free to use any sodium free seasonings to enhance taste.
My personal favorite is the brand "Mrs. Dash."

DIRECTIONS

1. Put frying skillet on medium heat.

2. Spray olive cooking spray until pan is completely covered.

3. Add the salt, pepper and any other seasonings you desire to both sides of the burger.

4. Place burger in skillet and cook on medium-high 4-6 minutes per side.

5. Place burger inside lettuce and top off with ketchup. Serve and enjoy!

CALIENTE TIP:
Add any flavor mustard and veggies for even more fun!

APPROXIMATE MACROS

Calories.....................265
Proteins..................22.5g
Fats.........................13g
Carbs....................7.8g

CHICKEN SPAGHETTI BUTTERNUT SQUASH

Serves 1

INGREDIENTS

2 cups of spiralized spaghetti squash (find it already pre-spiralized at local super market or use a spiral vegetable slicer)

1 cup of spinach

1 or 2 teaspoons of minced garlic

olive oil cooking spray

4 ounces chicken breast strips

DIRECTIONS

1. In a frying pan, spray olive oil cooking spray until pan is completely covered.

2. Place the squash and minced garlic into pan on medium-high for 5 minutes while stirring.

3. Put in sliced chicken strips into pan and cook on medium-high while stirring for another 5 minutes.

4. Add the spinach to pan, mix and stir for 1 minute. Serve and enjoy!

CALIENTE TIP:
Add some oregano for more flavor!

APPROXIMATE MACROS

Calories......................250
Proteins..................30g
Fats.........................6.3g
Carbs.....................23g

EGG WHITE SALAD LETTUCE WRAP

Serves 1

INGREDIENTS

5 boiled egg whites

1 large lettuce leaf. Use romaine lettuce or butter lettuce

1 tablespoon of either fat free mayo or miracle whip

1 teaspoon of low sodium salt

pinch of black pepper

3-5 sliced pre-cooked roasted red pepper strips

Seasoning: Feel free to use any sodium free seasonings to enhance taste. My personal favorite is the brand "Mrs. Dash."

DIRECTIONS

1. Boil eggs 7 minutes and peel.

2. Empty the yolk out of the eggs.

3. Chop all egg whites into a bowl and add 1 tablespoon of any of the dressings mentioned.

4. Add the salt and pepper with any additional seasonings you desire.

5. Mix well, then stir into the eggs until well incorporated.

6. Serve inside pieces of lettuce and then add slices of pepper on top. Enjoy!

CALIENTE TIP:
Add cherry tomatoes to enhance the crunch experience of the wrap!

APPROXIMATE MACROS

Calories.....................135
Proteins..................19g
Fats........................3.3g
Carbs.....................9.3g

CALIENTE BROTH SOUP

Serves 1

INGREDIENTS

2 cups of low fat/low sodium chicken broth

1 cup of chopped squash

½ cup of chopped leek

½ cup cilantro

½ cup chopped chicken breast

DIRECTIONS

1. In a soup pot, place broth and bring to a boil.

2. Add all the ingredients to the pot and put on medium-high for 5 minutes.

3. After the 5 minutes are up, put it on low heat and let it cook for 30 minutes. Serve and enjoy!

CALIENTE TIP:

Add mushrooms to compliment the meal!

APPROXIMATE MACROS

Calories.....................250
Proteins..................36g
Fats.........................2.5g
Carbs....................18g

SPICY TURKEY SPINACH

Serves 1

INGREDIENTS

4 ounces of cooked and sliced
low sodium turkey

2 cups of spinach

1 tomato

2 tablespoons of mustard (any flavor)

olive oil cooking spray

low sodium salt

Seasoning: Feel free to use any sodium
free seasonings to enhance taste.
My personal favorite is the brand
"Mrs. Dash."

DIRECTIONS

1. In a frying pan, spray olive oil cooking
spray until pan is completely covered.

2. Place spinach into pan and cook for
2 minutes.

3. Remove spinach, place on plate and
add turkey in addition to sliced tomato.

4. Top off with your favorite mustard,
a pinch of salt and your favorite
seasonings. Serve and enjoy!

APPROXIMATE MACROS

Calories.....................164
Proteins..................30g
Fats.........................1g
Carbs....................8.5g

CALIENTE TIP:
Add black olives for even
more flavor!

STEAK CAULIFLOWER RICE MEDLEY

Serves 1

INGREDIENTS

2 cups of cauliflower rice (find it already pre made at local super market)

olive oil cooking spray

2 cups of spinach

6 cherry tomatoes

3 ounces of lean skirt steak strips

DIRECTIONS

1. In a frying pan, spray olive oil cooking spray until pan is completely covered.

2. Place the cauliflower into pan on medium-high for 5 minutes while stirring.

3. Place steak strips into pan and cook on medium-high while stirring for another 5 minutes.

4. Add spinach, stir and cook for 1 minute.

5. Once done cooking, put on plate, and add cherry tomatoes. Serve and enjoy!

CALIENTE TIP:
Add 1 teaspoon of steak sauce for even more flavor!

APPROXIMATE MACROS

Calories.....................265
Proteins..................31g
Fats.........................6g
Carbs....................14g

TUNA FISH LETTUCE WRAP

Serves 1

INGREDIENTS

1 can of light tuna, canned in water (3oz.)

¼ cup onions chopped

½ tomato sliced

1 tablespoon of any of the following:
fat free mayo, miracle whip or mustard (any flavor)

2 large lettuce leaves. Pick any of the following: romaine lettuce or butter lettuce

Seasoning: Feel free to use any sodium free seasonings to enhance taste.
My personal favorite is the brand "Mrs. Dash."

DIRECTIONS

1. Thoroughly drain the tuna and place in medium size bowl.

2. Add ¼ cup of onions chopped.

3. Add 1 tablespoon of any of the dressings mentioned.

4. Mix well and then stir into the tuna until completely incorporated.

5. Serve inside lettuce and then add slices of tomatoes on top. Serve and enjoy!

APPROXIMATE MACROS

Calories......................130
Proteins....................20g
Fats..........................3.2g
Carbs.....................23g

BONUS: Sweet Treats

(If your goal is to lose weight, I recommend having these treats during the day or on cheat day)

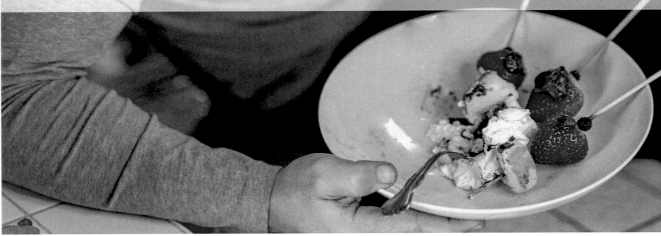

ANGEL FRUIT CAKE KABOB

Serves 1

INGREDIENTS

2 tablespoons of non-dairy Almond whip cream

1 slice/cup of angel food cake (50g)

1 cup of fresh sliced strawberries

½ cup of fresh blueberries

1 tablespoon of melted dark chocolate

1 skewer

DIRECTIONS

1. On skewer, add the cake and berries (load it up!)
2. Drizzle melted dark chocolate on top of the kabob. Serve and enjoy!

APPROXIMATE MACROS

Calories.....................248
Proteins..................5.5g
Fats.........................4.2g
Carbs.....................58g

HEALTHY PEANUT BUTTER & JELLY

Serves 1

INGREDIENTS

1 low calorie, lightly salted rice cake

2 tablespoons of powdered peanut butter
(I recommend PB2 brand)

1 tablespoon of grape sugar free jelly

DIRECTIONS

1. In a bowl, mix 1 to 2 tablespoons of water with 2 tablespoons of PB2.

2. Stir and mix until desired texture.

3. Place the peanut butter on top of rice cake and spread evenly.

4. Top it off with grape jelly.
Serve and enjoy!

APPROXIMATE MACROS

Calories.....................90
Proteins..................3.5g
Fats........................0.75g
Carbs....................15.5g

FRUIT CAKE

Serves 1

INGREDIENTS

1 low calorie, lightly salted rice cake

1 serving of JELL-O instant sugar free, fat free vanilla pudding

1 cup of mixed fruit (strawberries, blueberries, raspberries, blackberries, kiwi)

DIRECTIONS

1. Place JELL-O in a bowl once you have prepared it

2. Place 1 serving of JELL-O on top of rice cake (or as much as you can fit) and spread evenly

3. Top it off with fruits on top. Serve and enjoy!

APPROXIMATE MACROS

Calories......................155
Proteins..................2.5g
Fats.........................0.5g
Carbs......................37g

About The Author

Jason Rosell is an American/Spanish TV personality, artist, life coach, celebrity trainer, author, social media influencer and one of the world's premiere lifestyle and wellness experts and the founder of the award-winning global wellness brand, **Caliente Fitness**.

Rosell has successfully built his brand by helping thousands of women and men transform their mental, physical and spiritual mindsets, lose weight and achieve their wellness goals through his carefully curated life coaching, fitness & food programs and five-minute recipe books available through social media, television, internet and DVD.

Additionally, Rosell serves as a social media and branding strategist for individuals and companies seeking to revamp their online presence and social platforms.

His numerous television appearances include: The Steve Harvey Show, Jillian Michael's "Sweat INC", Hollywood Today Live, American Latino, All My Children, Saturday Night Live, VH1's I Love New York, I Love Money and many more.

JOIN JASON ON SOCIAL MEDIA FOR NEW CONTENT, DAILY **LIVE VIDEOS AND MUCH MORE!**

JASONROSELLLIVE

JASONROSELLLIVE

JASONROSELLLIVE

JASONROSELL

GET THE **MOST ADVANCED** FULL CUSTOMIZED MEAL, FITNESS PLANS AND WORKOUT VIDEOS!

The MIND RIGHT BODY TIGHT program is the most complete coaching, fitness and meal planning package for women & men wanting to get in the best shape of their life! And if you're looking for even more, check out my workout videos. I have helped 1000's of people transform their mind and body, are you next!?

THE #MINDRIGHTBODYTIGHT PROGRAM

WORKOUT VIDEOS

VISIT JASONROSELL.COM

DON'T HAVE THE FIRST YUMMY HEALTHY RECIPES BOOK? GO TO JASONROSELL.COM